# FAVORITE AUNTIE EMU

*poems by*

# Shoshana J. Coté

*Finishing Line Press*
Georgetown, Kentucky

# FAVORITE AUNTIE EMU

Copyright © 2016 by Shoshana J. Coté
ISBN 978-1-63534-070-9 First Edition
All rights reserved under International and Pan-American Copyright Conventions.
No part of this book may be reproduced in any manner whatsoever without written permission from the publisher, except in the case of brief quotations embodied in critical articles and reviews.

## ACKNOWLEDGMENTS

I am grateful for the guidance and encouragement of Professor Nancy Marashio and my formal and informal mentors at New England College. Special thanks go to my husband, Robert G. Coté.


Publisher: Leah Maines

Editor: Christen Kincaid

Cover Art: Ann St. Martin Stout   www.leavesarefree.tumblr.com

Author Photo: Robert G. Coté

Cover Design: Elizabeth Maines


Printed in the USA on acid-free paper.
Order online: www.finishinglinepress.com
          also available on amazon.com

Author inquiries and mail orders:
Finishing Line Press
P. O. Box 1626
Georgetown, Kentucky 40324
U. S. A.

# Table of Contents

Ordinary Ears ................................................................. 1
My Favorite Food .......................................................... 3
Ixobrychus ..................................................................... 4
I Don't Question ............................................................ 5
Stones ............................................................................ 6
Sarah Speaks ................................................................. 7
True Stories ................................................................... 8
Ars Poetica .................................................................... 9
Storm ........................................................................... 10
Night Whispers ........................................................... 11
F.A.E., babe, stands for Fetal Alcohol Effects
    and Favorite Auntie Emu ..................................... 12
Note to the Poet Paley ................................................ 13
Questions .................................................................... 14
For an Angry Teen and His Rap ................................. 15
We all have addictions, he said .................................. 16
Going Deaf .................................................................. 17
Wreck .......................................................................... 18
The Angel Blesses Jacob ............................................. 19
Lent .............................................................................. 20
What I Cover in a Basket ........................................... 21
So Many Fish .............................................................. 22
You want to know what it's like ................................. 23
Cento: Now that these words only resemble
    nothing in this life but hope ................................. 24

*These poems are intended to be read in sequence.*

**Ordinary Ears**
*Dedicated to Betty Klenck Brown*


From an island across the ocean
her call found me.
I was fifteen.

"This is Amelia Earhart Putnam.
Please help me.
Please—Hear me."

The shortwave radio caught her words—
I had to pull them in quick
or they'd be gone.

*Every word, Betty, pull it ashore and don't*
*stop to study it. Don't ask yourself if*
*it belongs there, just haul it in. Now.*

I was alone, but I did not stop writing.
Not for hours. When Daddy came home,
he took my notebook to the coastguard

but I was just an ordinary girl
with ordinary ears.
They laughed and turned away.

In the quiet gray of that first evening,
her last hours on earth
rippled around me.

In the nights that followed,
her voice rose and fell
on the waves that reached me in my sleep.

I wasn't a brave girl,
but to honor Miss Amelia
I learned to sail the skies.

A legacy was laid upon me;
I was not unwilling.
This old lady remembers.

**My Favorite Food**

My favorite color is tortoise-shell cat
in a patch of sun.

My favorite food is not
mollycoddle and milksop.

My favorite door is falling snow;
my favorite day is equinox.

My favorite season, skipping rope;
my favorite room, the roots of a word.

My favorite word is epi-oó-see-os,
hidden under mistranslation.

*Were not our hearts burning within us?*

My favorite story, spoken
on a road of seven miles.

Invisibility broken
before our baffled eyes.

My favorite dawn is esperanza;
my favorite day is equinox.

My favorite winter field
an empty page, holding its breath.

I hear my gentle dove coo:
*carry out the wish of the One who sent you.*

My favorite song is yes.

**Ixobrychus**

The burden of the bittern
is his self-assertion—
his self-assertion
with a bold drumbeat
deep and earthen.

deep and earthen,
sable of sound,
unfound—

in a veil so vertical
by the birder's boat
among twitch
and the reed-roar myth
of Ixobrychus.

## I Don't Question

I don't question what you are
any longer. You're in your kingdom.
You're like the blue jay—
imposing, waving his brilliant wings.
Nine minutes of strident bullying,
three minutes of silent indulgence.
Commonly I kneel beneath him,
performing the menial tasks:
digging, attending the flowers.
Commonly I listen from the steps
beside the flagstone path
until Kitty retreats, hoping
none have witnessed her defeat.
During all this, strength does not
abandon him.
Yet it surrounds me—
not as water the castle moat knows,
but as a colored bow in a cool mist.

**Stones**

Out of five or six in your palm,
one is always jagged and misshapen.
Forced to ruminate silence
among the smooth,
the liars dressed in silk.
And pebbles that looked paltry
are altered into beauty,
like new brides.

Out of five or six in your palm,
one is always jagged and misshapen.
No coat to hide its scrag.
Inside it,
your darkness.
Before it,
the deep.

Words without remission,
confidence without wisdom,
and sundered love
sunk there and staying down,
like dreadnaught with empty bodies
and no one to retrieve them.

## Sarah Speaks

I will not deny it. I stood in the shadow of the tent and listened. Would any woman choose otherwise, living in loneliness beneath a silent desert sun? With a good heart my husband served the three visitors, and they rewarded him with a promise.

I saw only that he pressed his face to the ground. One stranger repeated the words, and I also heard. Did I make a sound? For certain, I did not. But the stranger inquired of my laughter. A quick denial left my lips, yet he set the truth between us.

Who was this who could see behind the veil?
Who could perceive what flashed inside me?
Fear thickened my throat like sand.

My love sent me a look of understanding.
Then I knew his leaning into dust, and I drew hope
like water from a dark well.

It is true.
I did listen.
And I dared to believe.

## True Stories

In the chronicles of the Holy Land, you can read it for yourself:
approaching marauders changed the schedule of what was to be
a funeral.
Dead man cast into a nearby desert cave—
his friends said the quickest *Kaddish* ever.
But it so happened, the burial site was occupied
by a prophet.
Bones
thrown upon sacred bones,
and the man revived and stood upon his feet.

Imagine the surprise.

In Arizona, a certain man knelt and prayed.
"A saint," they said, "walking among us."
By the bones of Elisha,
who knows but that in touching that spot,
praying in that place,
we, too, can be revived.
Every time that Polish pope stepped off a plane,
he kissed the earth.
He kissed you, red earth, and I was twice blessed.
Arizona, little springs, I touched you and you touched back.

I am revived and stand upon my feet.

**Ars Poetica**

With a multicolored pen you ink the page
to which fall the seeds
from roots still unseen.

You choose the color, you choose the figure
that is freed
to slip among leaves.

What bright surround will frame the image
depends on the tree
that grounds you.

**Storm**

This is how some read the sky:
"Storm comin'—my elbow aches."
Stiffness in the knee, ankle pain.

I can't explain
how the air crackles
with anxiety.

I've been a long time learning
how the earth licks up the rain.
Something good is on the way—

some essential work.
The trick is to exercise
the trepidation.

Want to read the sky?
Move in that direction.

**Night Whispers**

*We stood in the antechamber
of her life,
settling the hues*

**F.A.E., babe, stands for Fetal Alcohol Effects
and Favorite Auntie Emu**

Time is a room where the lights are always
off. I crawl on my hands and knees,
a blind beggar hoping for pennies.
I build sentences with words

I can reach. "Last time" means
the day that just happened.
"A long time ago"
means more than a last time.

Counting backward makes my head hurt,
counting forward goes faster—
'til stuck at twenty-nine tells me
I'll die young.

**Note to the Poet Paley**

Your Chernobyl nightingales are never far away.

They've come to deliver a grace in this grief:
a boy drenched in chemical poison,
and an angel to bind us together.

I remain on call for tantrums from a teenager,
for medications gone awry,
for anxiety in glass-shattering metaphor.

Handed a key I cannot grasp,
wordless I awake.

I drag my pen across the desert
of this thirst,
the letters stumbling.

*Restore us, Lord,*
*like wadis in the Negev*
or grant us a telling
like that of nightingales.

**Questions**

I don't know how to ask this:
who takes care of those caught between?

Between can't make a sandwich
or can't make friends?

Can't draw a bunny
or can't draw conclusions?

Can't tie shoes
or tie an act to its result?

When, O Savior, will you deliver those in the between-world?
Between homes and between locks and between hopes.

**For an Angry Teen and His Rap**

Keep the sharp agony bound
in that dark desert cell,
where eden cannot enter.

Venom dwells in that pit.
It is with deception and charm
the true trance lies.

The mutation of word and wisdom—
rather, mutilation—
the disharmonic one still calls musical

plays you

**We all have addictions, he said**


Some smuggle theirs under
marshmallows or whipped cream.

Others tuck them inside a cookie.
Some ration out their poison daily.

At the neighbor's on the night that sparkles,
it's the best dessert. Darkest dark

is nearly unattainable,
like diamonds.

Still,

it can't be legal to want such sweetness:
to want fire like chocolate.

## Going Deaf

Subdue your hearing if you wish:
the grave has ears aplenty—
in which subsumes what assisted
the sounds upon the waves they traveled—
in which subsists what also stole you
out of sense
with a lie that you permitted
like the logic of two knives of bent
echo and jasper and rue.

**Wreck**

Every starboard bone groaned to haul your ship to harbor
after the disaster portside.

**The Angel Blesses Jacob**
> *"I will not let you go unless you bless me."*
> *(Genesis 32:27)*

Face it.
In a land where a man's name is his character,
you were a cripple from birth.

You win!
I remove from you the curse.
Of home and hip
you shall be dislocated.

Do not despise the pain.
Ignore
the wide-eyed stares of the innocent
and ill-mannered.

Bear up!
for with every uneven step
your bones will recollect
this was no imagined encounter.

**Lent**

Dolphins don't inhabit hope.
They assume it. The sea
never grows closer to its
beginning, only wider
in grief. It is our own absorption
darkening the deep.
So listen:
when you can distinguish tone
from tone and recognize
seagulls crying above your boat
as no sadder than the smiling
creatures below it, you'll begin
to fathom the lettered equation.

Give up guessing.

## What I Cover in a Basket

What I cover in a basket
climbs out through the weave,
ignoring my reluctance
and the day's decline

to greet me in the hour of praise
with song, or else scrabbling
at the chapel door I shut
against the beating
of my heart. Meaning

only this: Mercy is the wind
that knows its way
when the logic falls lame,

and whoever's glimpsed
the harvest winter tries to hide
is near to brushing unnumbered
wings above the altar.

## So Many Fish

All those eyes staring up at Simon—
staring through him, as if
they see the unseen inside him.

Such awareness of watching
washes over him together with
the empty space of sea now suddenly

full of created beings. Drops
of cold seawater trickle down his
exhausted arms, but this is not

what makes him tremble.
"Let me alone," says the fisherman,
tired from a night of catching nothing.

He sinks to his knees. "Leave me."
It makes him know his own emptiness,
this boat half-sunk with impossible

prosperity. Like the breaking nets,
his mind cannot contain
so many fish. They came—

from all over their watery world
they came to die
at the word of this rabbi.

Simon was not a listener,
he whose name implied
hearing and being heard.

But he was listening now,
and heard life in the words,
"Do not be afraid."

**You want to know what it's like**

but I can only tell you this:

Whale and diver hang in the blue expanse
regarding each other

Diver tries to hold steady—
she who is held in the gaze of a giant

Slowly
she opens her arms

This creature
could slay her in an instant

This creature
resplendent before her

inclines toward her / to speak Song

## Cento: Now that these words only resemble nothing in this life but hope

*Voice 1 (Child):*  When I lost my hearing, I began to see voices
fly in and out of windows.

*Voice 2:*  A child learns the world by putting it in his mouth.
Sifting down from a distant sky,
seven words for winter blend softly.

*Voice 3:*  Figures against which to measure a life.
So much attention required by dying.

*Voice 2:*  A brothel of leaves happily uniting
where the happiness of trees begins.

*Voice 1 (Child):*  Without a mirror I could not know
I suddenly heard Bach.

*Voice 4:*  Angels half-buried in a snowbank.
Press these words against your silence:
Leaf by leaf, step by step,
the evenings are my evidence.

*Voice 3:*  Figures against which to measure a life.
So much attention required by dying.

*Voice 2:*  This mathematical expression of light,
of lilac doused with shade,
cannot haunt you, child.
If you get lost in the woods,
all the arbitrary borders touching
that wildebeest of one's own rage,
that old enemy—distraction
flows north in a rhyme of night.

*Voice 1 (Child):*     We lived north of the future,
west of mist and morning haze,
numbers rubbed away.
It is always somebody's birthday
or the day of somebody's death.

*Voice 4:*     Leaf by leaf, step by step—
*Voice 3:*     So much attention required by dying.
*Voice 2:*     And seed scatters
the doves out of exile, shining.

*All speak, but not perfectly in unison:*     Deep blue dusk of days,
mussel-shell mosaics of wonder,
the boat spins slowly and
eternity is everywhere at once,
filling with rhyme.

Shoshana J. Coté grew up in Ohio. Her earliest memories are of laughter and good food while celebrating the Jewish holidays with family and friends. Even into her teen years, that spiritual and cultural environment produced in her a rich inner life. Whether at synagogue for a Sabbath service, at a weekend youth event or a summer camp, the prayers in Hebrew and English had a profound effect on her. Those prayers went forth in song, and the whole community sang together whether in joy or in sadness. The song leader (cantor) at the synagogue did not happen to be Jewish, but he could sing! The liturgical music planted seeds in her—melody, poetry and prayer all grew in the same garden.

On the other side of the family, she had Catholic grandparents who prayed quietly but often for their grandchildren. It is likely that those prayers—together with the devotional life she witnessed among Catholic friends—influenced her path.

Shoshana moved to New England in high school. It was at that time that she began to explore what had come down to her from both sets of grandparents. This exploration, which continued over a period of several years, deepened her love and gratitude for her Jewish heritage and introduced her to the liturgical world of prayer and song in Catholic and Orthodox churches.

Shoshana is an adjunct professor at a community college and a cantor at a local Catholic church. Her Hungarian-Jewish-Irish-Catholic roots nourish her poetic life and faith. She also belongs to the Secular Franciscan Order, a Catholic "third order" of men and women who live in the world but seek to follow the example of St. Francis of Assisi, St. Clare of Assisi and other Franciscans. She especially likes the example set by the Franciscans of the Holy Land. They have lived and worked peacefully among Jews, Muslims, and Christians (Catholic, Orthodox and Protestant) for 800 years.

Shoshana and her husband have two grown children and now share their home with an affectionate tortoise-shell cat named Flora and multiple happy fish.

www.ingramcontent.com/pod-product-compliance
Lightning Source LLC
LaVergne TN
LVHW041516070426
835507LV00012B/1604